THE NEXT LEVEL
Rise To New Heights
Master Your Journey

Recognize Where You Stand
Step Up To Your Next Level
And Take Charge

Chady Elias

The Next Level: Rise To New Heights
Master Your Journey
Recognize Where You Stand, Step Up To Your Next Level, And Take Charge.

This book is part of *In The Zone* Collection

For additional information contact ChadyElias.com

This Book is designed and intended for the individual, as a guide for self-help. No part of this book or any information contained within it constitutes professional treatment for any condition or clinical disorder, and is not considered an adequate substitute for professional or medical help. When distress in any form is experienced, one should seek professional guidance immediately.

ISBN 978-1-965668-00-9 (Paperback)

Chady LLC
Miami, FL
Printed 2025

To my amazing family
My beloved wife,
Ana Maria,

and my wonderful daughters,
Sophie and Zoie.

Your love, support, and inspiration
make everything possible.

~ Chady Elias

ACKNOWLEDGMENTS

A dear friend, after reading the book *Think and Grow Rich*, suggested forming a virtual mastermind group since we see each other in person almost every other week. On that week we were discussing how to recognize where we are and how to move forward. So, we created a WhatsApp mastermind group, and within the first week, she asked this question:

"How do i know what level i am and how to reach the next level?"

As you can see in the screenshot, I wrote a brief answer. Here it is:

"Happy day!!!

The brief answer is to approach the question from multiple perspectives:

1.Check with each aspect of you:

- **Spirit:** Reflect on your connection to your inner self and the universe. Are you feeling aligned with your purpose and values?

- **Heart:** Assess your emotional state. Are you feeling fulfilled and content? Are your relationships nurturing and supportive?

- **Body:** Evaluate your physical health. Are you taking care of your body through proper nutrition, exercise, and rest?

- **Mind:** Consider your mental well-being. Are you engaged in stimulating activities that challenge and grow

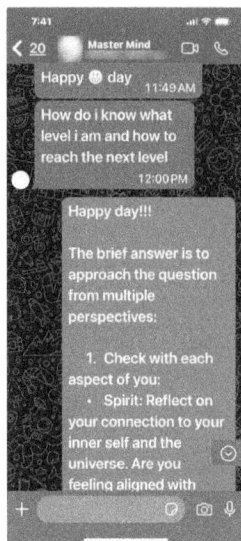

your intellect?

2.Check with each life you are living in:

- Public Life: How do you present yourself to the world? Are you authentic and true to yourself in public?

- Private Life: How do you interact with close friends and family? Are these relationships healthy and supportive?

- Secret Life: Are there aspects of your life that you keep hidden? Are these secrets necessary or are they hindering your growth?

- Internal Life: Reflect on your inner thoughts and feelings. Are you at peace with yourself? Are there unresolved issues you need to address?

When you understand what level you are at in each of these aspects, you can take steps to elevate yourself to a higher level by aligning your actions and decisions with the information you have about yourself."

And then I replied:
"Your question is a book by itself"

In that day, I started putting this book together.

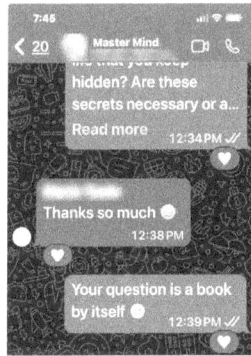

Special thanks and appreciation to
Marie Toole and Gabriella Villazon
for their friendship and support.

ABOUT THIS BOOK

The insights and exercises in "The Next Level" are rooted in my personal journey of meditation, life experiences, and the wisdom I've gained through creating art. Art has been my greatest teacher, offering lessons that extend beyond the canvas, shaping how I see the world and myself. Through this book, I've shared some of that wisdom with you, hoping it will inspire your own journey of growth.

For me, leveling up isn't a destination; it's a continuous process of self-evaluation and reflection. This practice has brought me immense growth, and by sharing these insights with you, I'm also taking my next step forward. This book is not just a guide; it's a part of my journey, an invitation for us both to rise to the next level together.

Snap, Share, and Post

At the end of each chapter, you will find "Snap, Post & Share" These are insights prepared for you to use as social media posts.

Here's how to use them: On your favorite social media platform, click the "+" button, take a picture, then post it, or save it to your phone to share.

You can also scan the QR code to download color and black-and-white social media content.

Social Downloads - TNL

My Tone In This Book

In business, you can't succeed unless you know your target audience. Once you do, you create an avatar to communicate with that audience.

For this book, my first avatars were my daughters and my wife. That's why at times, my tone may seem like I'm teaching while also sharing personal experiences and stories.

My second avatar is my family as a whole, including my future family, because family is important to me. The ideas and teachings in this book apply to creating, living, and maintaining every family.

My third avatar includes my friends and students since this book is about succeeding in both personal and professional life.

My fourth avatar is me. Yes, I wrote this book for myself too. I traveled the world on autopilot without a plan, just exploring and seeing what life would offer me. Life offered me my beautiful family, and now I'm giving back by sharing my learnings and experiences for the benefit of others—like you.

Additionally, as my next level involves succeeding in business and bringing prosperity to my life, which will impact my family, friends, and others, I wrote this book from a business perspective as well.

Creating a strong family and building a long-lasting business required me to understand myself and be aware of everything around me, both in the physical and metaphysical world.

No matter what stage of life you're in, you can always reach your next level. This book is an invitation and a guide for you to do just that.

SYMBOL MEANING

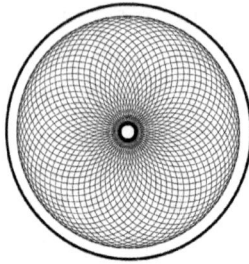

This symbol combines two sacred geometric forms: The Source and The Torus.

The large circle with the center circle represents The Source, symbolizing the origin and center of all things, with the central white dot signifying the core or focal point of this source.

This aspect of the symbol is also a representation of being "In The Zone," a state of flow where Spirit, Heart, Body, Mind are fully aligned, focused and in harmony.

The Torus mesh surrounding the central dot and filling the circle creating its border; signifies the continuous movement of energy, both spiritual and physical, within this zone.

Torus energy flows in a dynamic, circular pattern, symbolizing the harmonious exchange and balance between the spiritual and physical realms.

This combination of these two forms encapsulates the idea of interconnectedness, with energy continuously circulating through the source, embodying a state of unity and perpetual motion.

The Torus is roadmap for personal growth, symbolizes the cyclical nature of life's journey; where progress is not linear, but involves constant expansion and contraction.

In this framework, moments of success and "flow" represent the outward expansion, where everything seems to align and growth feels effortless.

These periods are balanced by inward contractions, where challenges, setbacks, or periods of confusion arise. Rather than viewing these as failures, the Torus teaches us that these dips are essential phases of growth, allowing us to turn inward, reassess, and realign with our core potential.

The continuous flow of energy within the Torus shows that even in moments of struggle, our connection to our inner source; the wellspring of creativity, strength, and potential; remains intact. It's a reminder that the energy is still flowing, even when it feels obstructed.

By understanding and applying this, we can embrace challenging times as opportunities for deeper self-awareness and personal refinement.

The Torus encourages us to cultivate practices like mindfulness, meditation, and self-reflection, which help us navigate the contractions with grace and patience.

The Torus is more than a symbol; it's a guide for understanding that personal growth is a dynamic, ongoing process, where every phase is necessary and part of a larger pattern that leads us back to our true self, the source.

POSITIVE AFFIRMATION

I Stand Up, I Step Up, I Take Charge

I am standing up
and I know my destination.

I am stepping forward
with confidence.

I hold the vision of the future me
in my Spirit, Heart, body, and Mind,
at all times.

I am taking charge
and achieving the vision
of the future me,
today.

~ Chady Elias

CONTENTS

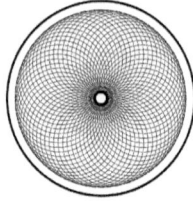

UNDERSTANDING LIFE LEVELS

Life is a journey filled with experiences that shape who we are and who we aspire to become. At the core of this journey are "life levels" distinct stages of growth and development unique to each person, influenced by their beliefs, experiences, and choices.

Imagine life as a video game, where each stage represents a different level you need to pass to reach the next. In each level, you face new challenges, learn new skills, and gain experience that helps you grow. Just like in a game, your life has levels that represent different stages of personal growth, learning, and development.

The Concept of Life Levels

The idea of life levels is rooted in the understanding that human growth is an ongoing process. Just as a video game character advances through levels by acquiring new skills, knowledge, and tools, we progress too through stages in our personal and professional lives. Each level represents a new phase of understanding, capability, and self-awareness, bringing us closer to our fullest potential.

The Uniqueness of Each Journey

While the concept of leveling up might suggest a straightforward path, the reality is that everyone's journey is unique. Some may find themselves quickly advancing in certain areas of life, while others may experience challenges that require them to revisit and strengthen foundational aspects of themselves. The beauty of life levels lies in their adaptability; they cater to the individual's needs, pace, and purpose.

Recognizing Your Current Level

One of the most important aspects of this journey is recognizing where you currently stand. Understanding your current level provides clarity on what areas of your life are thriving and which ones might need more attention. It's about being honest with yourself, acknowledging your strengths and limitations, and using this knowledge to set realistic goals for growth.

Personal and Professional Development

Once you have a clear understanding of your current level, you can more effectively navigate your personal and professional development. Recognizing these levels helps you prioritize your efforts, ensuring that you are focusing on the right areas at the right time. Whether it's advancing in your career, deepening your relationships, or cultivating a stronger sense of self, knowing your life level is the key to making intentional, impactful progress.

In this book, we will explore how to assess your current life level, understand the factors that influence it, and map out a path to reach the next level. By embracing this concept, you can take control of your growth journey, making conscious decisions that propel you forward in both your personal and professional life.

The Journey of Self-Discovery

Self-discovery is like going on an adventure to find out who you really are. Imagine you're a character in a video game, and you need to know your strengths, weaknesses, and what makes you happy. This is super important because it helps you figure out where you are in life, like understanding what level you're on in the game.

When you know where you stand, you can set goals that are right for you. It's like choosing the right mission in the game; one that's challenging but not impossible. If you don't know yourself, you might set goals that are too hard or too easy, and that can make you feel frustrated or bored.

Understanding yourself also helps you figure out what really matters to you. Maybe you love helping others, or you're passionate about art or science. Knowing this will guide you toward goals that make you feel fulfilled, like completing a quest that gives you a special reward.

Self-discovery is key to achieving personal fulfillment because it helps you set meaningful goals and move to the next level in your life, just like leveling up in a game by understanding your character and choosing the right challenges.

Note:_____

_____

_____

_____

_____

_____

Snap, Post & Share

The following social media posts are prepared for you to use on your platforms.

On your favorite social media, click + to snap a picture to post, or save and share.

You can also scan the QR code to download color and B&W versions of the posts.

Social Downloads - TNL

THE NEXT LEVEL

RISE TO YOUR NEW HEIGHTS

ChadyElias.com

Life Levels are distinct stages of growth and development that you experience on your unique journey. These levels represent challenges and opportunities for personal and professional growth.
Knowing where you currently stand, and at what level you are, you can navigate your path more effectively. This process of self-discovery helps you live a meaningful and fulfilling life.

I take control of my growth journey. I make conscious decisions to move forward.

Recognizing my life's level helps me prioritize my efforts and focus.

24

Everyone's journey is unique.

Life levels are catered to the individual's needs, pace, and purpose.

knowing
your
life level
is the
key to
making
intentional,
impactful
progress.

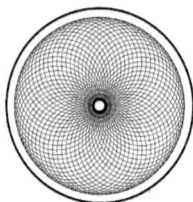

THE POWER OF YOUR BELIEF

Beliefs are like a pair of glasses that you wear all the time. They affect how you see the world and your life. If you believe something strongly, it can make you see things in a certain way, even if others might see them differently.

For example, if you believe that you're not good at math, you might start to see every math problem as super hard, even if it's not. This belief can make you feel stuck, like you're on a low level in a game that you can't get past. But if you believe that you can learn and get better, suddenly those problems might not seem so impossible, and you might start to level up.

The beliefs you hold shape your reality because they influence how you react to situations, how you feel about yourself, and even what you think is possible. If you believe that you can achieve your goals, you're more likely to try harder and not give up, which brings you closer to success.

However, sometimes your beliefs might not match up with what you really want in life. That's why it's important to examine them and see if they're helping you grow or holding you back. If you find a belief that's stopping you from reaching your dreams, you can work on reshaping it; like changing your glasses to see things more clearly. By aligning your beliefs with your goals, you can start to see new possibilities and move up to the next level in your life and business.

Multiple Beliefs

Beliefs come in many forms and categories; they are not just a single opinion on one thing. As I mentioned earlier, belief is the lens through which you see the world. To clarify, in each area of your life, you have a different lens to view that specific area. You have one lens for spirituality, another for religion, and similarly, different lenses for reality, relationships, health, wealth, and money. Even smaller concepts, like what food you eat, how you eat it, and why, are influenced by your beliefs.

Your beliefs are a multiverse that guides your life and decisions, both consciously and subconsciously. This is why I always suggest not accepting the status quo without examining it, just as I do in every aspect of my life. I consider myself the gatekeeper of my conscious and subconscious mind, the auditor of my beliefs. And I invite you to do the same.

The collective belief

Each country has its own customs; what seems respectful in one country may be disrespectful in another. This concept applies to religion, lifestyle, business, health, nutrition, and even race, ethnicity, and other areas; this is known as collective belief. Consciously or unconsciously, you belong to a collective belief system. You might consciously decide not to follow a certain belief, and by doing so, you're switching from one collective belief to another.

Every time you change your personal belief, you also shift into a new collective belief. You've likely heard sayings like, "Like attracts like," or "If you want to be healthy, be around healthy people." These slogans are invitations to join a new collective belief system.

The main point is to avoid entering a new collective belief by accident, as happened to me at various stages of my life.

Now, as the gatekeeper of my beliefs, I can control both my personal and collective beliefs, choosing which ones to adopt and which to let go of.

Nothing is real unless you believe in it.

Time is an illusion; it doesn't actually exist, but we created calendars and clocks, and we follow them. Some people follow the solar calendar, others follow the lunar calendar, and some follow a mix. Whatever calendar you choose, you do so because you believe it's the correct one.

When I was in primary school, I struggled to identify the names and numbers of the months, unconsciously I still do, because I was learning French. Saying some of the month names felt confusing for my analytical mind. For example, "September" means seven, but it's the nine month; "October" means eight, we use it as the tenth month; "November" means nine, and it's the eleventh month; and "December" means ten, yet it's the twelfth month. People decided to adopt this illogical calendar, we accepted it, and now we live by it.

This applies to political borders and countless other things we believe in but didn't decide for ourselves.

Some beliefs, like the names of the months, might seem harmless, but others have a more significant impact.

The reality around you is based on your beliefs. My beliefs are different from yours, which is why my reality is different from yours. The difference between our realities doesn't have to be good or bad; it's simply different.

My main point here is that your reality is shaped by the accumulation of beliefs you absorb unconsciously. By understanding this, you can change your reality by consciously choosing your beliefs. You can create and live in a new reality through conscious beliefs.

Self belief

I used to believe in everything that was passed down to me from my parents and their parents before them. These beliefs shaped my understanding of the world, but over time, I began to question them. Challenging those inherited beliefs allowed me to discover my own truths, ones that resonate deeply with who I am today. This journey of self-discovery has led to the most profound change in my belief system: embracing my full potential, both as a spiritual being and as a human. Though I'm still striving to reach that level, I am more aligned with my true self than ever before.

I invite you to do the same. Challenge your beliefs, whether they seem small or significant. By consciously examining and reshaping them, you can build a belief system that truly supports you on your journey. Your beliefs are like a compass, guiding you toward your next level. By aligning them with your true self, you'll not only grow but also unlock your full potential.

Tools and Exercises

A- Belief Inventory Exercise

This exercise helps you become aware of the beliefs that shape your worldview and influence your decisions. By identifying which beliefs are empowering and which are limiting, you can start to reshape those that may be holding you back

List Your Beliefs:

Write down at least 10 statements that you believe to be true about yourself, others, and the world. For example: "I believe hard work always pays off," or "I believe people can't be trusted." Then answer the questions under each belief.

Belief 1

_____

- Where did this belief come from? (e.g., family, experiences, culture)

_____

- How strongly do I hold this belief?

_____

- Does this belief empower me, or does it hold me back?

_____

Belief 2

- Where did this belief come from? (e.g., family, experiences, culture)

- How strongly do I hold this belief?

- Does this belief empower me, or does it hold me back?

Belief 3

- Where did this belief come from? (e.g., family, experiences, culture)

- How strongly do I hold this belief?

- Does this belief empower me, or does it hold me back?

Belief 4

- Where did this belief come from? (e.g., family, experiences, culture)

- How strongly do I hold this belief?

- Does this belief empower me, or does it hold me back?

Belief 5

- Where did this belief come from? (e.g., family, experiences, culture)

- How strongly do I hold this belief?

- Does this belief empower me, or does it hold me back?

Belief 6

- Where did this belief come from? (e.g., family, experiences, culture)

- How strongly do I hold this belief?

- Does this belief empower me, or does it hold me back?

Belief 7

- Where did this belief come from? (e.g., family, experiences, culture)

- How strongly do I hold this belief?

- Does this belief empower me, or does it hold me back?

Belief 8

- Where did this belief come from? (e.g., family, experiences, culture)

- How strongly do I hold this belief?

- Does this belief empower me, or does it hold me back?

Belief 9

- Where did this belief come from? (e.g., family, experiences, culture)

- How strongly do I hold this belief?

- Does this belief empower me, or does it hold me back?

Belief 10

- Where did this belief come from? (e.g., family, experiences, culture)

- How strongly do I hold this belief?

- Does this belief empower me, or does it hold me back?

B- Categorize Beliefs:

Divide your beliefs into two categories: empowering beliefs and limiting beliefs.

	Empowering Beliefs	Limiting Beliefs.
1		
2		
3		
4		
5		
6		
7		
8		
9		
10		
12		
13		
14		
15		

2. Behavior and Belief Connection

Understand how your core beliefs influence your daily actions and decisions.

By connecting your actions to your beliefs, you gain insight into how your beliefs guide your behavior, helping you see patterns that might need adjustment for your personal growth.

Practice:

1- **Choose a Recent Decision**: Think about a recent decision you made, whether big or small (e.g., choosing a career path, how you responded in a conflict).

2- **Analyze the Decision:** Write down what you did, why you did it, and what you believed about the situation that led to your decision.

3- **Link Beliefs to Actions:** Identify which of your core beliefs influenced this decision. For example, if you avoided a difficult conversation, it might be linked to a belief that conflict is always negative.

4- **Reflect:** Ask yourself if this belief served you well in that situation. How might your decision have been different if you held a different belief?

Decision 1

_____

Analyze:_____

Link:_____

Reflect:_____

Decision 2

_____

Analyze:_____

Link:_____

Reflect:_____

Decision 3

_____

Analyze:_____

Link:_____

Reflect:_____

Decision 4

_____

Analyze:_____

Link:_____

Reflect:_____

Decision 5

_____

Analyze:_____

Link:_____

Reflect:_____

Decision 6

_____

Analyze:_____

Link:_____

Reflect:_____

Decision 7

_____

Analyze:_____

Link:_____

Reflect:_____

Decision 8

_____

Analyze:_____

Link:_____

Reflect:_____

Decision 9

_____

Analyze:_____

Link:_____

Reflect:_____

3. Challenging Limiting Beliefs

Identify and challenge beliefs that may be limiting your potential. This exercise helps you transform limiting beliefs into more constructive ones, enabling you to make decisions that align better with your goals and values.

1- Identify a Limiting Belief: Look at the list of limiting beliefs from the Belief Inventory above choose the ones that you feel significantly impacts your life.

2- Examine the Evidence: Write down evidence that supports this belief and evidence that contradicts it. For example, if you believe "I'm not good at public speaking," write down times when you struggled and times when you succeeded.

3- Reframe the Belief: Create a new, empowering belief that is more balanced and realistic. For instance, "I'm improving at public speaking with practice."

4- Take Action: Test this new belief in real life. Challenge yourself to a situation that allows you to act on your new belief and observe the outcome. Remember "NOW" is the wright moment.

Example:

Identify: I'm not good at public speaking.

Evidence: I struggled with my speech yesterday. Before yesterday my speech was good.

Reframe: I'm improving at public speaking with practice

Action: I am practicing now and I am searching for a venue to speak at.

Limiting Belief 1

_____

Evidence:_____

Reframe:_____

Action:_____

Limiting Belief 2

_____

Evidence:_____

Reframe:_____

Action:_____

Limiting Belief 3

_____

Evidence:_____

Reframe:_____

Action:_____

Limiting Belief 4

_____

Evidence:_____

Reframe:_____

Action:_____

Limiting Belief 5

_____

Evidence:_____

Reframe:_____

Action:_____

Limiting Belief 6

_____

Evidence:_____

Reframe:_____

Action:_____

Limiting Belief 7

_____

Evidence:_____

Reframe:_____

Action:_____

Limiting Belief 8

_____

Evidence:_____

Reframe:_____

Action:_____

4. Visualization of Future Self

Align your core beliefs with your desired future self by visualizing how your beliefs shape your future. This exercise helps you align your current beliefs with your long-term goals, setting you on a path toward becoming the person you want to be.

1- Imagine Your Future Self: Close your eyes and picture yourself five or ten years from now, living your ideal life. Think about where you are, what you're doing, and how you feel.

2- Identify Beliefs: Consider what beliefs this future version of you holds. For example, if your future self is successful in your career, what beliefs have helped you get there?

3- Compare to Present Beliefs: Compare these future beliefs with your current ones. Identify any differences or gaps.

4- Create an Action Plan: Write down steps you can take to start adopting the beliefs of your future self today. For instance, if your future self believes in lifelong learning, commit to a habit of reading or taking courses regularly.

1) Imagine you are in the future:

_____

What beliefs have helped you get there?

_____

What is the difference between your todays belief and your future belief?

_____

What steps are you taking to adopt the belief that is going to take you to the future you?

_____

2) Imagine you are in the future:

_____

What beliefs have helped you get there?

_____

What is the difference between your todays belief and your future belief?

_____

What steps are you taking to adopt the belief that is going to take you to the future you?

_____

_____

3) Imagine you are in the future:

_____

What beliefs have helped you get there?

_____

What is the difference between your todays belief and your future belief?

_____

What steps are you taking to adopt the belief that is going to take you to the future you?

_____

_____

Snap, Post & Share

The following social media posts are prepared for you to use on your platforms.

On your favorite social media, click + to snap a picture to post, or save and share.

You can also scan the QR code to download color and B&W versions of the posts.

Beliefs act like a lens through which you see the world, shaping your reality and influencing how you approach challenges. Strong beliefs can either empower you or hold you back, depending on how they align with your goals. If you believe in your ability to grow and improve, you're more likely to overcome obstacles and achieve success. It's important to examine and reshape beliefs that limit you, allowing you to see new possibilities and progress in life.

ChadyElias.com

45

Everything is Real,

Unless you don't believe in it.

ChadyElias.com

46

Your beliefs are the lenses of your life.

Adjust them, and you'll see how limitless your potential truly is.

Stuck?

it's time to level up your beliefs and unlock new challenges.

ChadyElias.com

What you believe defines your path.

Align your beliefs with your goals, and step into your future.

49

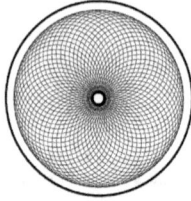

UNDERSTANDING WHERE YOU STAND
PERCEPTION, PERSPECTIVE, & REALITY

When you think about reality, perception, and perspective, it's important to know that nothing stays the same. Everything is constantly changing, just like the quote by *Heraclitus*: **"No man ever steps in the same river twice. For it's not the same river, and he's not the same man."** Every moment, every place you visit, and every experience you have can change how you feel, what you know, and what you believe. These changes shape how you see reality, how you perceive the world, and what your perspective is.

Reality

Reality is how things really are, no matter how you feel about them or what you think. It's like the truth that doesn't change based on someone's opinion.

Take gravity, for example. Whether you believe in it or not, gravity is real. It's the force that keeps everything grounded and stops us from floating into space. Even if someone has never heard of gravity or doesn't understand it, it's still there, working all the time. This is what reality means; something that's true no matter what anyone thinks.

Perception

Perception is how you see and understand the things around you. It's based on your senses, your experiences, and what you believe. Perception isn't the same for everyone; it can be totally different depending on who you are and what you've gone through.

Imagine you and a friend go to a restaurant. You might think the dim lights and soft music make it cozy and cool. But your friend might find it to dark and old-fashioned. You're both in the same place, but you see it differently because of your perceptions. This shows how personal and unique perception can be.

Perspective

Perspective is your overall way of looking at things. It's shaped by your background, your experiences, and what you value. Perspective is bigger than just one moment or one thing you see—it's how you understand the world as a whole.

Let's say you're having an argument with a friend. One person might see it as a problem that needs a logical solution, like figuring out who's right and who's wrong. Another person might be more focused on the emotions involved, wanting to make sure everyone feels understood. Each person's perspective shapes how they deal with the situation. When you try to see things from different perspectives, you're looking at the problem from all angles, which can help you find a solution that works for everyone.

Understanding reality, perception, and perspective can help you navigate changes in life, allowing you to grow and make better decisions in life and business.

Where do you stand and how to go forward?

Imagine something happened to you in the past that hurt you. How do you know it hurt? Through your memories of the event. But what if you took that memory and looked at it from a different perspective? What if you realized that what you thought happened wasn't exactly how it went down? By doing this, you could heal from that past hurt, and in a way, change your past by seeing it in a new light.

A Story of Perception

When you were a kid, you were walking with your dad on a nice, sunny afternoon. You were having a good time until suddenly, your dad grabbed your arm really tight, causing you pain, and shoved you to the side. It hurt a lot, and after that day, you started to believe that your dad had a bad temper and could be hurtful. Because of this, you decided to avoid walking with him from then on.

Understanding Reality and Perspective

Fifteen years later, you're talking with your mom, and she tells you a story about how your dad once saved you from getting hit by a car. You're confused and say, "I don't remember that!" Your mom asks if you remember when your hand was sore for a week and you were upset, refusing to go on walks with your dad. You do remember that. Then your mom explains that the day your dad grabbed you was the day he saved you from that car. Suddenly, everything clicks—you realize your dad wasn't being mean or losing his temper. He was actually protecting you.

By learning this, you've completely changed how you see that memory. What you once thought was a hurtful moment is now a moment where your dad showed how much he cared about you. This new understanding changes not only how you see the past but also how you might act in the future. Maybe now, you're open to going on walks with your dad again, knowing that he loves you and was never angry with you.

This story shows how perception, reality, and perspective are connected. What you believe about an event can change when you gain new information or look at it from a different angle, helping you heal and grow.

Tools and Exercises

Sometimes, the way we see things isn't always how they really are. Our perceptions, perspectives, and understanding of reality can get mixed up because of our experiences, emotions, or even the people around us. Here are some tools and exercises to help you take a closer look at how you view the world and remember events so you can get a clearer picture of what's really going on.

Using the following tools and exercises, will help you to deal with your perceptions, perspectives, and understand of reality that influence your life and business. The more you practice, the better you'll get at seeing things clearly, which can help you make more informed choices and feel more in control of your life.

1. The Reality Check Journal

This exercise helps you become more aware of how your perceptions might be influencing your view of reality, giving you the chance to see things more clearly.

Start questioning your daily perceptions and perspectives by writing them down and reflecting on them.

Instructions

1.Daily Entry: Each day, pick one event or interaction that stood out to you and write it down in your journal.

2.Describe Your Perception: How did you perceive the event? What emotions did you feel? What thoughts ran through your mind?

3.Question It: Ask yourself if there could be another way to see this event. Could someone else perceive it differently? Write down any alternative perspectives.

4.Reflect: Look back at your entries at the end of the week. Do you notice any patterns in how you perceive things? Are there any assumptions you made that might not be true?

Practice:
Day 1:

What event or interaction that stood out to you today?

_____

How did you perceive the event?

_____

What emotions did you feel?

_____

What thoughts ran through your mind?

_____

Is there could be another way to see this event?

_____

Could someone else perceive it differently?

_____

Day 2:

What event or interaction that stood out to you today?

_____

How did you perceive the event?

_____

What emotions did you feel?

_____

What thoughts ran through your mind?

_____

Is there could be another way to see this event?

_____

Could someone else perceive it differently?

_____

Day 3:

What event or interaction that stood out to you today?

_____

How did you perceive the event?

_____

What emotions did you feel?

_____

What thoughts ran through your mind?

_____

Is there could be another way to see this event?

_____

Could someone else perceive it differently?

_____

Day 4:

What event or interaction that stood out to you today?

_____

How did you perceive the event?

_____

What emotions did you feel?

_____

What thoughts ran through your mind?

_____

Is there could be another way to see this event?

_____

Could someone else perceive it differently?

_____

Day 5:

What event or interaction that stood out to you today?

_____

How did you perceive the event?

_____

What emotions did you feel?

_____

What thoughts ran through your mind?

_____

Is there could be another way to see this event?

_____

Could someone else perceive it differently?

_____

Day 6:

What event or interaction that stood out to you today?

_____

How did you perceive the event?

_____

What emotions did you feel?

_____

What thoughts ran through your mind?

_____

Is there could be another way to see this event?

_____

Could someone else perceive it differently?

_____

Day 7:

What event or interaction that stood out to you today?

_____

How did you perceive the event?

_____

What emotions did you feel?

_____

What thoughts ran through your mind?

_____

Is there could be another way to see this event?

_____

Could someone else perceive it differently?

_____

Week 1:

Do you notice any patterns in how you perceive things?

_____

_____

_____

_____

_____

_____

Are there any assumptions you made that might not be true?

_____

_____

_____

_____

_____

_____

What did you learn about your perceptions, perspectives, and reality this week?

_____

_____

_____

_____

_____

_____

Week 2:

Do you notice any patterns in how you perceive things?

_____

_____

_____

_____

_____

_____

Are there any assumptions you made that might not be true?

_____

_____

_____

_____

_____

_____

What did you learn about your perceptions, perspectives, and reality this week?

_____

_____

_____

_____

_____

_____

2. Mind Map Your Memories

This tool helps you see that memories aren't always as clear-cut as they seem. By breaking them down and examining them, you can gain new insights and possibly change how you feel about the past.

Explore your memories from different angles to understand how your perspective might have shaped them.

Instructions

1.Choose a Memory: Pick a significant memory that you think has impacted you a lot.

2.Create a Mind Map: Start with the memory in the center and draw branches for different aspects, such as "How I felt," "What I thought," "What others might have felt," and "What was actually happening."

3.Fill It In: Under each branch, write down details about the memory. Try to see it from multiple perspectives, including those of others involved.

4.Reevaluate the Memory: Look at your mind map and see if there's anything new you noticed. Does this change how you feel about the memory? Would you remember it differently now?

Note: _____

_____

_____

_____

_____

_____

Practice:

Write a memory

_____

How did I felt? In the past

_____

What I thought? In the past

_____

What others might have felt? In the past

_____

What was actually happening? In my today's view

_____

Write details about that memory? From todays perspective

_____

Is there anything new you noticed?

_____

Does this change how you feel about the memory?

_____

Would you remember it differently now?

_____

3. Perspective Swap

This exercise helps you develop empathy and see that there's often more than one side to every story. It can also help you navigate conflicts better by understanding where the other person is coming from.

Practice seeing situations from someone else's point of view to broaden your perspective.

Instructions

1.Pick a Situation: Think of a recent argument, disagreement, or challenging situation.

2.Write Your Perspective: Write down how you saw the situation, including your feelings, thoughts, and actions.

3.Swap Perspectives: Now, imagine you're the other person in the situation. Write down how they might have seen it. What were their feelings, thoughts, and actions?

4.Compare and Reflect: Compare the two perspectives. How different are they? What did you learn by seeing it from the other person's point of view? How might this understanding change how you act in the future?

Note: _____

_____

_____

_____

_____

Practice:

1. From your memory

Write a situation:

_____

How did you see the situation?

_____

What was your feeling?

_____

What were your thoughts?

_____

What actions did you take?

_____

2. Now imagine you're the other person in the situation

Write down how they might have seen the same situation

_____

What were their feelings?

_____

What were their thoughts?

_____

What were their actions?

_____

3. Compare the two perspectives

How different are your perspectives?

_____

What did you learn by seeing it from the other person's point of view?

_____

How might this understanding change how you act in the future?

_____

4. Reality vs. Interpretation

This exercise helps you separate your emotions and assumptions from the actual facts, allowing you to see situations more clearly and make better decisions.

Separate what actually happened from how you interpreted it to see things more objectively.

Instructions

1.Describe an Event: Think of an event that upset or confused you and write down exactly what happened, sticking to the facts (e.g., "I got a B on my test").

2.Identify Your Interpretation: Write down what you thought about the event and how it made you feel (e.g., "I'm not smart enough").

3.Challenge Your Interpretation: Ask yourself if your interpretation is the only way to see it. What other explanations are there? Could your feelings be based on something else?

4.Rewrite the Story: Based on this reflection, rewrite the story with a more balanced view of what happened and how you can move forward.

Practice:

Write an event that upset or confused you

_____

What are your thoughts about this event?

_____

How this event made you feel?

_____

Is your interpretation to this event is the only way to see?

_____

What other explanations are there?

_____

Could your feelings be based on something else?

_____

Rewrite the story with a more balanced view

_____

How can you move forward?

_____

What lesson did you learn?

_____

Snap, Post & Share

The following social media posts are prepared for you to use on your platforms.

On your favorite social media, click + to snap a picture to post, or save and share.

You can also scan the QR code to download color and B&W versions of the posts.

THE NEXT LEVEL

Perception is only mine

Perspective is a wider point of view.

Reality is constant.

ChadyElias.com

Look at the past with fresh eyes.

A new perspective can rewrite your future.

Every moment changes me,

with new perspectives, and understanding I change every moment.

Your perspective shapes your journey.

Shift your view, and you will find your right paths forward.

69

Perception is the way you interpret and understand the world, shaped by your senses, experiences, and beliefs. It varies from person to person, making each individual's view of the same situation unique. For example, what feels cozy to one person might seem unappealing to another. Perception highlights the personal and subjective nature of how we see things.

Perspective is your broad view of the world, shaped by your background, experiences, and values. It influences how you interpret situations, like whether you focus on logic or emotions during a conflict. Different perspectives lead to different approaches to the same problem. Seeing things from multiple perspectives can help you find well-rounded solutions that work for everyone.

Reality is the unchanging truth that exists regardless of personal beliefs or opinions. Like gravity, it remains constant and affects everyone, whether they understand or acknowledge it. Reality is independent of how we feel or think about it. It represents the true nature of things, beyond perception or belief.

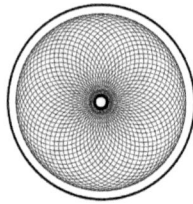

ALL ASPECTS OF ME
SPIRIT, HEART, BODY, AND MIND

There have been times in my life where I felt completely stuck. It was like no matter what I did, I couldn't move forward in life, creativity, business, or relationships. Then I realized something huge, if I didn't know myself, I'd never get anywhere. That's when it hit me that self-awareness is the key to personal growth.

When I figured out my strengths, weaknesses, values, and passions, I could set goals that actually mattered to me and chase after them with confidence. Knowing myself better helped me make smarter decisions, stay motivated, and deal with life's challenges in a way that made sense.

Feeling stuck usually means it's time to look deeper into yourself. It's like life's way of telling you to hit pause and think about where you are and where you want to go. Taking the time to dig into your inner world can help you uncover things like hidden fears, patterns, and dreams that are driving your actions. It's not always easy, but this kind of self-reflection can give you a lot more clarity and make you feel more empowered.

In this chapter, we're diving into the different parts

that make up who you are; your spirit, heart, mind, and body. By looking within, we can explore emotions, perceptions, and beliefs that go beyond fear and build self-confidence.

To become more self-aware, start by focusing on the present moment and realizing that life is always changing. This mindset can open up endless possibilities and help you redefine your future. In my experience, the best place to start on your self-awareness journey is with your own existence.

But figuring out where to start isn't easy. "Beginning" is a pretty big word, right? I didn't know if I should start with the beginning of the universe, the beginning of my spirit, or the day I was born.

Then, one day, the answer came out of nowhere. I was standing in front of my mirror, brushing my hair. Suddenly, I looked into my own eyes in the reflection and asked, **"Who are you?"** And just like that, the answer started to form. Even though I had studied philosophy and theology, I had never seen it this clearly before. Here's what I realized:

René Descartes famously said, **"I think, therefore I am."** Building on that idea, when we exist, we exist as some form of energy.

According to the first law of thermodynamics, *Albert Einstein* said, **"Energy cannot be created or destroyed; it can only be changed from one form to another."** If our existence is a form of energy, then that means we're eternal beings who just keep transforming.

This insight opens up a whole new way to think about our beliefs in the divine, the universe, where humanity came from, and what we're capable of. It makes you wonder about how our spiritual essence is connected to the energy of the universe, and how that shapes the way we see existence and our potential.

If we think of energy as representing our spirit or soul, then our body is our physical form, and our mind is what lets us say, **"I think, therefore I am."** So, the core of who we are comes down to this: **"The essence of my reality is that my spirit has a heart, my heart has a body, my body has a mind."** My spirit is my eternal energy, my heart connects me to my spirit, my body protects my heart, and my mind helps me make sense of it all.

The Spirit

The spirit is like a form of energy, and as Einstein said, "Energy cannot be created or destroyed; it can only change from one form to another." This means that your spirit, as energy, is eternal; it can't be destroyed. Everyone has a spiritual side, which is a sign that there's more to life than just what we can see or touch. This also means believing in the soul and in something that goes beyond just the physical body.

To reconnect with your spirit and make it a part of your daily life, try saying this affirmation whenever you need:

THE NEXT LEVEL

"It's easy for me, right now, to recognize and be aware that I am spirit and I have a heart, body, and mind. With appreciation and gratitude, I affirm this truth."

The Heart

I think of the heart as a seed planted in the middle of my body. Its roots grow down into my foundations, and its leaves reach up toward higher wisdom. Our heart is what connects us to the universe. Because we love life, we keep our hearts beating. We should all practice heartfulness, which means being super aware of our heart's actions and waking up to its full potential. It's about paying attention to the emotions, intentions, and energy that come from our hearts. When we do this, we can tap into the heart's wisdom and compassion, which helps us feel more empathy, build resilience, and find inner peace. It also strengthens our connection to the spirit, the divine, and other people, bringing together the physical and spiritual parts of our lives.

To bring your heart into your daily routine, you can repeat this affirmation whenever you need:

THE NEXT LEVEL

"It's easy for me, right now, to recognize and be aware that my heart connects me to the spiritual world and others. I acknowledge that my heart is protected by my body and mind. With appreciation and gratitude, I affirm this truth."

ChadyElias.com

The Body

The body is the physical part of who you are—the part that interacts with the outside world. It's important to realize that your body is an essential part of your existence and that it protects your heart, which is the connection to your spirit. To keep your body in your daily awareness, you can use this affirmation whenever you need:

THE NEXT LEVEL

"It's easy for me, in my body, to recognize and be aware that I have a heart that connects me to my spirit, and my body protects my heart. I acknowledge my mind, which keeps me safe in the world. I affirm this with appreciation and gratitude."

ChadyElias.com

The Mind

The mind is what lets you know you exist. Like René Descartes said, "I think, therefore I am." Every person has a mind, which is the part that thinks, is conscious, and processes everything. The mind is crucial for survival because it helps us understand reality and adjust to it, keeping the connection between the body and spirit strong through the heart.

To stay aware of what your mind does in your daily life, try saying this affirmation whenever you need:

THE NEXT LEVEL

"It's easy for me, in this moment, to recognize and be aware that my mind is protecting me, and I have a body that holds my heart, and a heart that connects my spirit. With appreciation and gratitude, I affirm this truth."

ChadyElias.com

All Aspects of Me

People usually say, "You are body, mind, and spirit." But that made me think that I should start with the body. Now I know that I'm a spirit with a body, not the other way around, so from now on, my spirit comes first. The heart is the first organ to develop when a baby is forming, and because our connection to others comes from the heart, I realize that my heart connects me to my spirit, and my body protects my heart. My mind keeps my body safe. So, the heart is the connection, and the mind is the protection. From now on, I'll say **"Spirit, Heart, Body, and Mind"** instead of the usual "body, mind, and spirit."

This new way of looking at things recognizes how the spiritual, emotional, physical, and mental sides of you are all connected. These four parts together make up the core of how you see, experience, and understand your reality.

Understanding this is crucial because it shows you that you are an eternal, powerful being who can create and achieve anything you set your mind to. If you want to get into the zone, this awareness is key to getting there faster.

If you don't agree with me, that's okay. I invite you to think about your own beliefs and write them down so you can keep them in mind for your self-awareness journey. Just know that my belief in existence comes from a spiritual perspective, not a religious one.

Tools and Exercises

Spirit: Meditation for Spiritual Awareness

Strengthen your connection with your spirit by tapping into your inner energy and the greater universe.

Meditation:

1. **Find a Quiet Space:** Sit or lie down in a peaceful environment where you won't be disturbed.

2. **Focus on Your Breath:** Close your eyes and take deep, slow breaths. Inhale through your nose, hold for a few seconds, and exhale through your mouth.

3. **Visualize Your Energy:** Imagine a glowing light within you, representing your spirit. Visualize it growing brighter with each breath, filling your entire being with warmth and peace.

4. **Affirmation:** Repeat, "I am an eternal being of light and energy, connected to the universe." Let this affirmation sink in as you continue breathing deeply.

5. **Reflect:** Spend a few minutes after your meditation reflecting on any insights or feelings that arose. Journal your thoughts to deepen your connection.

Note:

_____

_____

_____

_____

_____

Heart: Heartfulness Practice

Cultivate a deep awareness of your emotions and connect with your heart's wisdom.

Practices:

1.**Heart-Centered Breathing:** Place one hand over your heart and close your eyes. Breathe slowly and deeply, focusing on the rise and fall of your chest.

2.**Emotional Check-In:** Ask yourself, "How am I feeling right now?" Name your emotions without judgment. Acknowledge them as they are.

3.**Gratitude Reflection:** Think of three things that you're grateful for today. As you focus on each one, allow your heart to swell with appreciation.

4.**Affirmation:** Silently or aloud, say, "My heart is the center of my being, connecting my spirit to my body, guiding me with wisdom and love."

5.**Action:** Commit to one heart-centered action today, such as offering kindness to someone or practicing self-compassion.

Note:

_____

_____

_____

_____

_____

Body: Mindful Movement

Reconnect with your physical self by engaging in mindful movement and body awareness.

Practices:

1.**Stretching Routine:** Start your day with gentle stretching. Focus on how each movement feels, noticing any areas of tension or relaxation.

2.**Mindful Walking:** Go for a walk in nature or around your neighborhood. Pay attention to how your body moves, the sensation of your feet touching the ground, and the rhythm of your breathing.

3.**Body Scan:** Lie down in a comfortable position. Starting from your toes and working up to your head, mentally scan each part of your body. Notice any sensations, tensions, or areas of comfort.

4.**Affirmation:** While scanning your body, repeat, "My body is strong, capable, and the vessel of my spirit, heart and mind."

5.**Healthy Habit:** Choose one small, healthy habit to incorporate into your daily routine, such as drinking more water, eating mindfully, or prioritizing sleep.

Note:

_____

_____

_____

_____

_____

Mind: Mental Clarity and Focus

Enhance your mental clarity and strengthen your mind's ability to focus and process information.

Practices:

1.**Daily Journaling:** Spend 10 minutes each day writing down your thoughts, worries, and ideas. This helps clear mental clutter and allows for deeper reflection.

2.**Mindful Reading:** Select a book or article that interests you. As you read, focus entirely on the content, absorbing the information fully without distraction.

3.**Puzzle Time:** Engage in activities that challenge your mind, such as solving puzzles, playing strategy games, or learning something new. These exercises stimulate cognitive function and creativity.

4.**Affirmation:** Throughout the day, remind yourself, "My mind is clear, focused, and capable of great understanding."

5.**Mindful Breaks:** Schedule short breaks throughout your day to clear your mind. During these breaks, practice deep breathing, stretch, or simply relax to reset your focus.

Holistic Reflection

At the end of each day, take a few moments to reflect on how you engaged with your spirit, heart, body, and mind.

Consider how these practices influenced your thoughts, feelings, and actions. This holistic approach will help you become more self-aware and balanced in all aspects of your life.

Snap, Post & Share

The following social media posts are prepared for you to use on your platforms.

On your favorite social media, click + to snap a picture to post, or save and share.

You can also scan the QR code to download color and B&W versions of the posts.

THE NEXT LEVEL

My Spirit is connected to my Heart

My body protects my Heart.

My Mind protects My Body

ChadyElias.com

My Spirit, Heart, Body, & Mind Are In Harmony

My heart is the bridge between my spirit and my body.

I cultivate heartfulness to strengthen my connection.

I Am Spirit

Having Heart, Body, & Mind

88

Your
Heart
is to
connect

**Your
Mind
is to
protect**

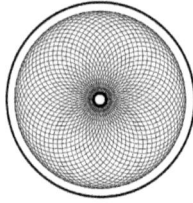

EXPLORING YOUR MULTIPLE LIVES PUBLIC LIFE, PRIVATE LIFE, SECRET LIFE, & INTERNAL LIFE

Even when you think you know yourself well, others still see you differently. Your friends, family, and even strangers all have their own unique way of perceiving you. Sometimes, even the people who are closest to you don't see you the way you see yourself. This idea shows that we live our lives in different layers or dimensions, each with its own perception, perspective, and reality.

These layers "public life, private life, secret life, and internal life" make up the different parts of who you are. Each one gives others a different view of you, which can lead to multiple versions of "you" that exist in the world.

Think of these different layers as concentric circles, with each one fitting inside the other. Your public life is the outermost circle, while your internal life is at the center. These layers overlap and influence each other, creating a complex picture of who you are.

Understanding these different dimensions of life can help you see how your identity is shaped through various layers of perception. It shows that there are many sides to who you are, and that each one plays a role in how you experience the world and how the world experiences you.

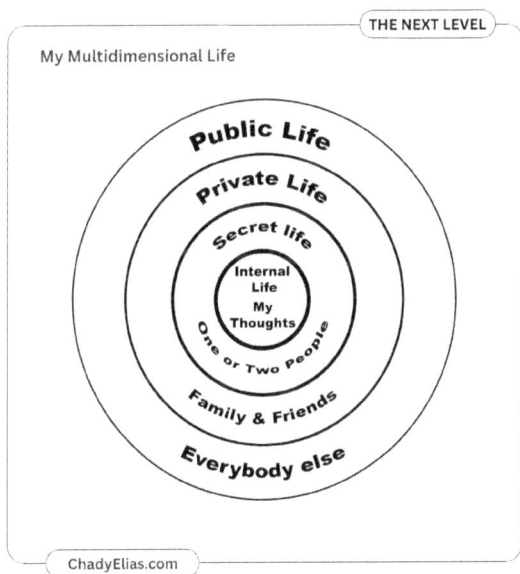

THE NEXT LEVEL

My Multidimensional Life

Public Life
Private Life
Secret life
Internal Life
My Thoughts
One or Two People
Family & Friends
Everybody else

ChadyElias.com

Public Life: How People See You

The outermost layer is your public life. This is how everyone else; like acquaintances, coworkers, teachers, and even strangers; see you. It's the part of you that's on display to the world, influenced by how you present yourself and how others view you in different situations.

In your public life, people see you based on what society expects and the roles you play. This is how you show yourself to the world; your actions, how you look, and how you interact with others. But here's the thing: each person sees you a little differently, depending on how they know you. This means that your public image isn't the same for everyone; it changes depending on who's looking.

This idea is kind of like a graph showing how different people see different parts of you in their own lives, and how you're viewed in society overall. It's all about the mix of opinions from people who know you well, kind of well, or not at all.

1.My View of Myself (Central Circle)
This is how you see yourself—your thoughts, feelings, and the way you understand who you are. It's the core of your identity and the most important perspective.

2.My Colleague's View of Me (Triangle)
This shape represents how your coworkers see you. Their view is shaped by how you act at work, how you perform, and how you interact with them professionally.

3.My Neighbor's View of Me (Rectangle)
This is how your neighbors see you. They form their opinion based on how you behave in your neighborhood, like whether you're friendly, quiet, or

involved in community activities.

4.My Social Media Friend's View of Me (Oval)

This shape shows how your friends on social media see you. Their view is influenced by what you post, how you interact online, and the kind of image you present on your favorite Social platforms.

5.The General Public's View of Me (Pentagon)

This is how the wider public sees you. It's based on any public activities you do, how you appear in public places, and the overall reputation you have among people who don't know you personally.

These different shapes represent the various ways people see you, depending on how they know you. They remind us that who we are isn't just one thing; it's a mix of all these different perspectives. This idea highlights how our identity changes depending on the situation and who's looking at us.

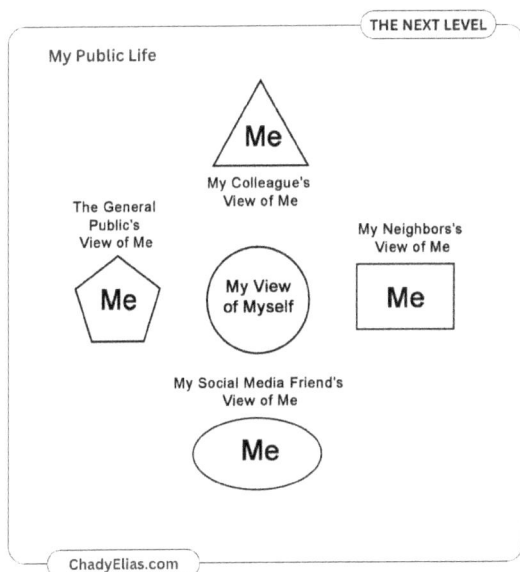

THE NEXT LEVEL

My Public Life

Me

My Colleague's
View of Me

The General
Public's
View of Me

Me

My View
of Myself

My Neighbors's
View of Me

Me

My Social Media Friend's
View of Me

Me

ChadyElias.com

Private Life: How Your Close Ones See You

This is the side of you that your family and close friends see. They know you better than the general public does, but they don't know everything; only what you choose to share with them.

Your private life is all about your relationships with family and close friends; the people who know you best. Even though these relationships are close, everyone still sees you a little differently, depending on how they know you and what they've experienced with you. This means that even those who are closest to you might not see you exactly as you see yourself.

Here's how different people in your private life might see you from their own perspectives:

1.My View of Myself (Circle in the Center)
This is how you see yourself—your thoughts, feelings, and the way you understand who you really are.

2.My Partner's View of Me (Triangle on the Left)
This shows how your boyfriend, girlfriend, or partner sees you. Their view might be different from how you see yourself or how others see you.

3.My Mom's View of Me (Rectangle on the Bottom)
This represents how your mom sees you. Her view is shaped by all the things she's been through with you, her expectations, and your relationship with her.

4.My Dad's View of Me (Pentagon on the Right)
This shape stands for how your dad sees you. His perspective offers another unique view of who you are.

5.My Siblings' View of Me (Oval on the Top)

This is how your brothers or sisters see you. Their views are influenced by the experiences you've shared growing up together and the dynamics within your family.

These shapes and labels show that each person in your life has their own way of seeing you. When you put all these perspectives together, they create a more complete picture of who you are. The image reminds us that our identity isn't just one thing; it's made up of all these different views, shaped by the relationships and experiences we have with the people close to us.

Understanding these different perspectives can help you see yourself in a new way and realize that who you are is complex and multi-dimensional, shaped by how others perceive you in your private life.

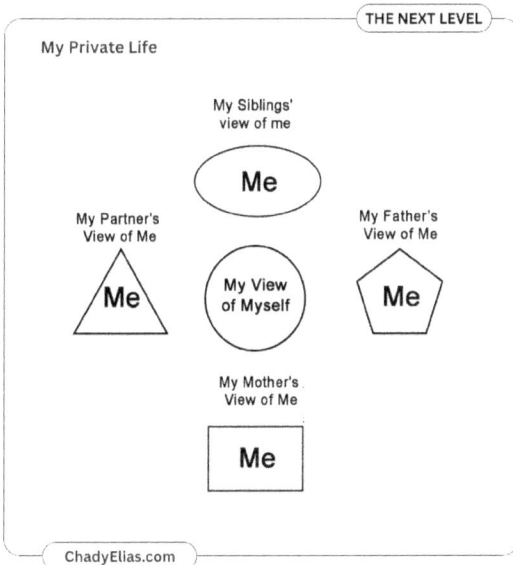

THE NEXT LEVEL

My Private Life

My Siblings' view of me

Me

My Partner's View of Me

Me

My View of Myself

My Father's View of Me

Me

My Mother's View of Me

Me

ChadyElias.com

Secret Life: The Parts of You That Few People Know

This part of you is known only to one or two people you trust completely. These are the things you share with just a select few, adding another dimension to who you are.

Your secret life is all about the things you keep hidden from most people. You might share some of these secrets with one or two people, but even then, they don't see the full picture of who you are. No matter how close someone is to you, they still see you through their own perspective, which means they can't fully understand everything about you.

Here's how this concept works:

1.My Partner's View of Me (Triangle Symbol)
Even if you share some of your secrets with your boyfriend, girlfriend, or a close friend, their view of you is still incomplete. They might know a lot about you, but they can't see every side of who you are.

2.My View of Myself (Eye in Circle Symbol)
This represents how you see yourself, including your deepest thoughts, feelings, and secrets. You know yourself better than anyone else, but even your own view is sometimes influenced by how you think others see you.

This idea shows that even the people closest to us can't fully understand everything that's going on inside us. Our secret life is a part of who we are that remains hidden, and only we can truly know it all.

My Secret Life

My Partner's
View of Me

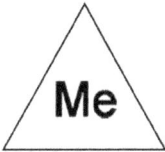

Me

My View
of Myself

97

Internal Life: The Secret World Inside Your Head

The deepest part of who you are is your internal life. This is where all your private thoughts, emotions, and the conversations you have with yourself live.

Inside your head, there's a whole world that only you know about. This includes your deepest thoughts, feelings, and beliefs; stuff you don't share with anyone else.

This is the most private part of who you are. Even though you might think you know yourself really well, your self-image is always changing. Who you are right now isn't exactly who you were even a few moments ago, and this constant change is a huge part of your internal life.

Here's how this idea looks:

My View of Myself (Overlapping Shapes)
This shows how you see yourself. It's like a mix of different shapes (like circles, squares, and triangles) that overlap. These shapes represent the many sides of your personality and how you're always growing and changing. Your view of yourself isn't just one thing; it's complicated and keeps evolving as you experience new things and think more about who you are.

This idea highlights that knowing yourself is a journey. It's about understanding that who you are inside is always shifting, and that's okay. It's part of what makes you, you.

Across different parts of life, everyone deals with the challenge of figuring out who they are. Recognizing the difference between what's inside you and how others see you, while accepting that you're always changing, is key to really understanding yourself.

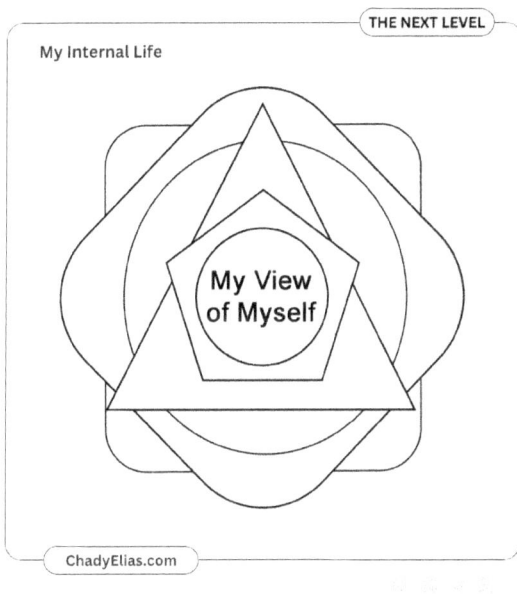

THE NEXT LEVEL

My Internal Life

My View
of Myself

ChadyElias.com

Tools and Exercises

Figuring out who you are in different parts of your life can be tricky, but it's super important. These exercises will help you look at your Public Life, Private Life, Secret Life, and Internal Life to see where you're strong and where you might want to grow.

1. Public Life: The Social Mirror

Step 1: Think about how you act in public; at work, online, or around people who don't know you well.

What do you think others see when they look at you?

_____

_____

_____

Step 2: Ask a few friends, classmates, or work friends what they think your best qualities are. Do they match what you thought?

_____

_____

_____

Step 3: Write down the qualities they mentioned. Compare them to how you see yourself.

Are there any surprises?

_____

_____

_____

2. Private Life: The Circle of Trust

Step 1: List the people who are closest to you, like your best friends or family members. Next to each name, write down what you think they would say is your biggest strength and your biggest weakness.

Friends or Family Members	Your biggest strength	Your biggest weakness.

Step 2: Now, actually ask them! Compare what they said to what you wrote. How close were you?

Friends or Family Members	Your biggest strength	Your biggest weakness.

Step 3: Think about any differences between what you thought and what they said. This can show you areas where you're strong in your close relationships and where you might want to grow.

3. Secret Life: The Truth or Reflection

Step 1: Think about the secrets you keep; things only one or two people know about you. What are these secrets, and why do you keep them?

_____

_____

_____

_____

Step 2: Reflect on whether keeping these secrets makes you feel strong or stressed. Is there anyone you trust enough to share more of your secrets with, or are you comfortable keeping them to yourself?

_____

_____

_____

_____

Step 3: Write down your thoughts on whether these secrets are helping or holding you back. This will help you understand if sharing more or less would be better for you.

_____

_____

_____

_____

4. Internal Life: Who Am I, Really?

Step 1: Take a quiet moment and think deeply about who you are when no one else is around.

1.What are your biggest dreams that you don't share with anyone?

_____

_____

_____

_____

2.What are your biggest fears that you don't share with anyone?

_____

_____

_____

_____

3.What are your biggest feelings that you don't share with anyone?

_____

_____

_____

_____

Step 2: Write down how you see yourself right now.

1. What are your strengths?

_____

_____

_____

2. What are your struggles?

_____

_____

_____

3. how you've changed over the past year?

_____

_____

_____

Step 3: Think about how you want to grow.

1. What do you want to work on internally?

_____

_____

_____

2. Write down a few goals for understanding yourself better

_____

_____

_____

Snap, Post & Share

The following social media posts are prepared for you to use on your platforms.

On your favorite social media, click + to snap a picture to post, or save and share.

You can also scan the QR code to download color and B&W versions of the posts.

THE NEXT LEVEL

My internal life is my secret world inside my head.

ChadyElias.com

Your secret life is all about the things you keep hidden from most people.

Even those who are closest to you might not see you exactly as you see yourself.

Public Life is how you show yourself to the world.

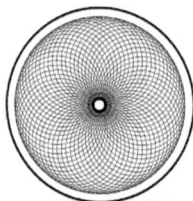

LEVELING UP

How to Set Realistic Goals for Your Next Level

Setting goals can be a game-changer, but it's important to do it right so you actually reach them. Here's a step-by-step guide to setting goals that are realistic and really mean something to you. We're going to talk about SMART goals and how to make sure your goals line up with who you are—your Spirit, Heart, Body, and Mind, as well as the different parts of your life.

Step 1: Get Clear on What You Want

1.**Perception:** Start by thinking about how you see yourself and your life right now. What do you believe is possible for you? Your beliefs shape your reality.

2.**Perspectives:** Look at your life from different angles. How do you see yourself in your Public Life, Private Life, Secret Life, and Internal Life? What areas need attention or change?

3.**Reality:** Now, focus on what's real. What do you truly want to achieve? Be honest with yourself about where you are and where you want to go.

Step 2: Use the Power of Belief

1.Your beliefs are super powerful. If you believe you can achieve something, you're already halfway there. Make sure your goals align with what you truly believe is possible.

2.If you find yourself doubting, remind yourself that you can grow and change. Strengthen your belief by visualizing your success and how it will feel to achieve your goal.

Step 3: Align Your Goals with All Aspect of You

1.**Spirit:** Think about what your spirit or soul truly desires. What goal will make you feel more connected to who you really are?

2.**Heart:** Consider your emotions and passions. What goal excites you or fills your heart with joy?

3.**Body:** Don't forget your physical self. What goals will help you feel stronger, healthier, or more at peace in your body?

4.**Mind:** Finally, think about your mental state. What goals will challenge your mind, help you grow intellectually, or give you clarity?

Step 4: Make Your Goals SMART

1.**Specific:** Be clear about what you want to achieve. Instead of saying, "I want to get better," say, "I want to improve in this specific area of my life."

2.**Measurable:** Make sure you can track your progress. How will you know when you're getting closer to your goal? What milestones can you hit along the way?

3.**Achievable:** Your goal should be challenging but possible. Don't set yourself up for failure by aiming too high too soon. Take steps that you know you can handle.

4.**Relevant:** Make sure your goal really matters to you. It should align with your Spirit, Heart, Body, and Mind, and help you grow in your Public, Private, Secret, or Internal Life.

5.**Time-bound:** Give yourself a deadline. This helps you stay focused and motivated. Set a specific time frame for reaching your goal.

Step 5: Break It Down

Big goals can feel overwhelming, so break them down into smaller steps. What can you do today, this week, or this month to move closer to your goal?

_____

Step 6: Stay Flexible

Life changes, and so can your goals. If something isn't working, don't be afraid to adjust your plan. Keep checking in with yourself to make sure your goals still align with who you are and what you want.

_____

Step 7: Reflect and Celebrate

As you work on your goals, take time to reflect on your progress. How have your perceptions, perspectives, and reality shifted? Celebrate your wins, no matter how small. This keeps you motivated and shows you how far you've come.

Your goals should be a reflection of who you are and who you want to become. By aligning your goals with your Spirit, Heart, Body, and Mind, and by making them SMART, you're setting yourself up for success. Remember, you have the power to shape your reality and reach the next level in any area of your life.

Strategies and Daily Practices for Reaching Your Goals

Reaching your goals isn't just about setting them; it's about taking daily action and staying consistent, even when things get tough. Here's how you can start making progress towards your goals by focusing on key areas of your life; your Spirit, Heart, Body, and Mind; as well as how you're perceived in your Public, Private, Secret, and Internal Life.

1. Start with the Power of Belief

Daily Practice: Every morning, remind yourself of your goal and believe that you can achieve it. Say to yourself, "I have the power to make this happen." The more you believe in yourself, the more motivated and focused you'll be.

Strategy: Create a vision board or write down your goals and keep them where you can see them every day. This keeps your belief strong and reminds you of why you're working towards these goals.

2. Shift Your Perception, Perspectives, and Reality

Daily Practice: Take a few minutes each day to reflect on how you see yourself and your goals. Are there any negative thoughts holding you back? Challenge them and replace them with positive, empowering thoughts.

Strategy: Journal your thoughts and feelings regularly. This helps you track your progress and see how your perception and perspective are changing. It also helps you stay in tune with your reality, ensuring you're on the right path.

3. Nurture Your Spirit, Heart, Body, and Mind

- **Spirit:**

Daily Practice: Spend some quiet time each day connecting with your inner self. This could be through meditation, prayer, or simply sitting quietly and reflecting.

Strategy: Find something that makes your spirit feel alive, like spending time in nature, practicing gratitude, or connecting with something bigger than yourself. Make this a regular part of your routine.

- **Heart:**

Daily Practice: Focus on your emotions and how they align with your goals. Ask yourself, "Does this goal make my heart happy?" If not, consider adjusting it.

Strategy: Surround yourself with positive influences—people, music, books—that uplift your heart and keep you emotionally connected to your goals.

- **Body:**

Daily Practice: Take care of your body by staying active and eating well. A healthy body supports a healthy mind and spirit.

Strategy: Set aside time each day for physical activity, whether it's a walk, workout, or stretching. Listen to your body and give it what it needs to stay strong and energized.

- **Mind:**

Daily Practice: Challenge your mind by learning something new every day. This keeps you sharp and ready to tackle obstacles.

Strategy: Read, watch, or listen to something that expands your knowledge or challenges your thinking. Keep your mind open and curious.

4. Balance Your Public, Private, Secret, & Internal Lives

- **Public Life:**

Daily Practice: Be mindful of how you present yourself to others. Stay true to who you are, but also be aware of how your actions align with your goals.

Strategy: Choose your social interactions wisely. Spend time with people who support your goals and bring out the best in you.

- **Private Life:**

Daily Practice: Deepen your connections with family and close friends. Share your goals with them, and let them be a source of encouragement.

Strategy: Set aside time for meaningful conversations and activities with the people who matter most. These relationships can be a strong foundation for your success.

- **Secret Life:**

Daily Practice: Protect your personal secrets and inner thoughts. Not everything needs to be shared. Focus on what truly matters to you.

Strategy: Have one or two trusted individuals you can confide in when you need support. Choose wisely who you let into this inner circle.

- **Internal Life:**

Daily Practice: Spend time reflecting on your inner world—your thoughts, beliefs, and feelings. This is where your true self resides.

Strategy: Regularly check in with yourself. Ask, "How am I feeling? What do I need right now?" This self-awareness keeps you grounded and aligned with your goals.

5. Embrace Consistency, Resilience, and Adaptability

- **Consistency:**

Daily Practice: Commit to small, consistent actions every day. Whether it's 10 minutes of meditation, a quick workout, or writing down your thoughts, these small steps add up.

Strategy: Create a daily routine that supports your goals. Stick to it, even when you don't feel like it. Consistency builds momentum.

- **Resilience:**

Daily Practice: When challenges arise, remind yourself that setbacks are part of the journey. Keep going, even when it's tough.

Strategy: Develop a mantra or phrase that motivates you to push through tough times. For example, "I am strong enough to overcome this."

- **Adaptability:**

Daily Practice: Be open to change. If something isn't working, don't be afraid to adjust your plan.

Strategy: Regularly review your progress and be flexible with your approach. Sometimes, the path to your goal might look different than you expected, and that's okay.

Final Thoughts

Progressing towards your goals is a journey that requires daily effort, belief in yourself, and a willingness to adapt. By nurturing all aspects of yourself; your Spirit, Heart, Body, and Mind; and balancing your life's different dimensions, you can move closer to your goals each day. Stay consistent, be resilient, and keep growing. You've got this!

6. Creating a Vision of Your Next Level

Imagine a version of yourself that's leveled up—someone who's confident, accomplished, and living their best life. This is your next level, and to get there, you need to create a vivid vision of who you want to become and what you want to achieve. This isn't just about dreaming; it's about visualizing your future self so clearly that you can almost feel it. Let's dive into how you can do this by tapping into the power of belief, perception, perspectives, and the realities of your Spirit, Heart, Body, and Mind.

Step 1: Believe in Your Vision

Start with Belief: The first step in creating a vivid vision is believing that it's possible. You have to trust that you can become the person you want to be and achieve the things you desire. Without belief, your vision is just a fantasy. But with belief, it becomes a goal you're committed to reaching.

Step 2: Visualize Your Next Level

Close Your Eyes and Imagine: Picture yourself at

your next level. Who are you? How do you act? What does your life look like? This isn't just about surface-level stuff like clothes or status. Think deeper—how do you feel? What kind of energy do you give off? What kind of impact are you making on the world?

Use All Your Senses: When visualizing, don't just see it —hear it, feel it, even smell it. The more senses you involve, the more real your vision becomes. For example, imagine the sound of your voice when you're speaking confidently, or the warmth in your heart when you're doing something you love.

Step 3: Align Your Spirit, Heart, Body, and Mind

Spirit: In your vision, connect with your spirit. This is the part of you that's timeless and powerful. Ask yourself, "What does my spirit need to feel fulfilled?" This could be a sense of purpose, connection to something greater, or simply peace and contentment.

Heart: How does your heart fit into this vision? Your heart is where your emotions and passions live. In your next level, your heart should be full—of love, joy, and compassion. Visualize yourself feeling these emotions deeply.

Body: See your body as strong, healthy, and capable. It's the vehicle that will carry you through your journey. Imagine yourself taking care of it, treating it with respect, and feeling great in your own skin.

Mind: Your mind is where your thoughts and beliefs live. At your next level, your mind is sharp, focused, and positive. Picture yourself thinking clearly, making wise decisions, and staying mentally strong no matter what challenges arise.

Step 4: Consider Your Public, Private, Secret, and Internal Lives

Public Life: How do you want the world to see you? In your vision, think about how you present yourself to others—how you interact with acquaintances, colleagues, and even strangers. What kind of energy do you bring into the room? Visualize yourself being confident, authentic, and true to who you are, no matter the setting.

Private Life: Now, think about your relationships with close friends and family. In your next level, these relationships should be strong and supportive. Visualize yourself having deep, meaningful conversations, sharing your thoughts and feelings, and being there for the people who matter most.

Secret Life: Even at your next level, you'll have parts of yourself that you only share with one or two people —or maybe no one at all. In your vision, these secrets are safe and well-guarded. Picture yourself being honest with the people you trust, while still keeping certain things just for you.

Internal Life: Finally, focus on your inner world—your thoughts, beliefs, and self-awareness. At your next level, you should feel at peace with who you are. Visualize yourself understanding your own mind, being kind to yourself, and continuously growing and evolving.

Step 5: Live Intentionally

Bring Your Vision to Life: Visualization is powerful, but it's only the beginning. To make your vision a reality, you need to live intentionally. This means making choices every day that align with your vision. Ask yourself, "Is what I'm doing right now helping me become the person I want to be?"

Stay Committed: There will be times when it's hard to stay on track, but remember; your vision is worth it. Keep believing, keep visualizing, and keep moving forward. The more you live in alignment with your vision, the closer you'll get to making it real.

Your next level is within reach, but it starts with a clear vision and a strong belief in yourself. By visualizing who you want to become and what you want to achieve, and by aligning your Spirit, Heart, Body, and Mind, you're setting the stage for an incredible transformation. Remember, it's not just about dreaming; it's about taking action and living with intention every day. Keep your vision in your heart, stay true to yourself, and watch as you evolve into the person you're meant to be.

Embodying Growth: Living Your Best Life

You've come a long way in your journey, and now it's time to fully step into the new version of yourself. It's not just about reaching goals; it's about embodying the changes you've made and living your best life every single day. This is where all your hard work, belief, and vision come together.

Step 1: Live in Alignment with Your Highest Potential

Stay True to Your Vision: Remember the vivid vision you created for your next level? Now it's time to live in alignment with that vision. Every decision you make, every action you take, should reflect the person you've become and the life you want to lead. Keep asking yourself, "Is this choice helping me live my best life?"

Listen to Your Spirit, Heart, Body, and Mind: Stay connected to all parts of yourself—your Spirit, Heart, Body, and Mind. When you're in tune with each of these, you'll be better equipped to make decisions that are right for you and stay on the path to continuous growth.

Step 2: Keep Reassessing and Adapting

Growth is Ongoing: Growth doesn't stop once you reach a goal. It's an ongoing process. Regularly check in with yourself to see how you're doing. Are you still on track with your vision? Have your goals changed? Are there new challenges you need to face? Be honest with yourself, and don't be afraid to adjust your path if needed.

Be Open to Change: Life is unpredictable, and things don't always go as planned. Embrace change as part of your journey. When something unexpected happens, see it as an opportunity to learn, grow, and evolve. The more adaptable you are, the more you'll be able to navigate life's ups and downs while staying true to your vision.

Step 3: Embody the New You Every Day

Practice What You've Learned: Everything you've learned so far; about belief, visualization, living intentionally, and more; should be part of your daily life. Don't let these lessons fade away. Keep practicing them, and let them guide you in everything you do.

Stay Committed to Your Growth: Growth is a lifelong

journey. Even when you feel like you've reached a new level, there's always more to discover and achieve. Stay committed to your personal growth, and keep pushing yourself to reach even higher levels of potential.

Live Your Best Life

Living your best life means embracing everything you've learned, staying true to yourself, and constantly striving to grow. It's about being the person you want to be, every single day. It's about living with purpose, passion, and intention. And most importantly, it's about finding fulfillment in the journey, not just the destination.

Remember, you have the power to create the life you want. Keep believing in yourself, keep visualizing your next level, and keep embodying the growth you've achieved.

Your journey is yours to shape, and with every step, you're becoming the best version of yourself.

Live fully, grow continuously, and never stop reaching for your highest potential.

Snap, Post & Share

The following social media posts are prepared for you to use on your platforms.

On your favorite social media, click + to snap a picture to post, or save and share.

You can also scan the QR code to download color and B&W versions of the posts.

THE NEXT LEVEL

My Beliefs Shape My Reality.

ChadyElias.com

I Believe In My Vision of Myself.

125

I Set SMART Goals

S pecific

M easurable

A chievable

R elevant

T ime-bound

ChadyElias.com

I align my goals with my Spirit, Heart, Body, & Mind.

WHAT IS NEXT?

The Next Level in Creativity

A Bonus free E-book

As you embark on your journey through *The Next Level*, you'll discover powerful insights about growth, transformation, and aligning with your highest potential. But what if you could take this even further; unlocking your deepest creative flow and limitless innovation?

To help you expand even more, I'm offering you a **free bonus eBook: *The Next Level in Creativity*.**

This exclusive guide dives into **how creativity is an innate, spiritual force within you**, how to break through creative blocks, and how to align your **Spirit, Heart, Body, and Mind** to reach new heights of self-expression. Whether you're an artist, entrepreneur, or simply looking to expand your creative thinking, this eBook will help you step into your **full creative power**. Download it now and **take your creativity to the next level!**

Scan this QR code to download your Free E-book Bonus

The Next Level in Creativity - Free Bonus

Master Your Journey

After reading this book, your next level is to live it! You've taken the first step by expanding your mindset, aligning with your purpose, and elevating your awareness. Now, it's time to put everything into action and immerse yourself in the next phase of your journey. I invite you to join *Master Your Journey* - a transformative community designed to help you unlock your full potential, eliminate confusion, and create a life of fulfillment and success. This isn't just a group; it's a movement of like-minded individuals stepping into their highest selves.

In *Master Your Journey*, you'll gain access to cutting-edge tools, live coaching, and powerful courses designed to align your thoughts, actions, and energy with success.

With your own AI Virtual Coach; trained with my expertise; you'll receive tailored guidance every step of the way.

The time for transformation is NOW. No more waiting, no more "someday"; *your next level begins today.*

Scan this QR code to know more and to Start Your Free 7-Day Trial

MASTER YOUR JOURNEY

Books:

PUBLICATIONS

Explore my other books and workbooks that dive deeper into creativity, personal growth, and self-discovery. Scan the QR code to check them out.

Blogs:

I regularly write blogs that explore creativity, human experiences, and art. Join me in these thought-provoking discussions by reading my latest posts. Scan the QR code to start reading.

BLOG

Coaching:

COACHING

Explore and live the endless horizons of achievement. There are no boundaries to what one can achieve. Scan the QR code to start the conversation with me.

Speaking & Podcasting:

Scan this QR code to book me for speaking engagements and podcast interviews.

BOOK ME

ABOUT THE AUTHOR

Chady Elias is a visual artist, creativity coach, business strategist, hypnotherapist, and NLP practitioner based in Miami, Florida. With a Master's in Fine Arts and extensive experience in creativity, personal development, and transformational coaching, Chady helps individuals and businesses break creative barriers, align with their purpose, and achieve extraordinary growth.

Chady's work is rooted in the belief that self-awareness, innovation, and strategic transformation are the keys to reaching the next level; whether in art, business, or personal success. Through his artwork, coaching programs, corporate training, workshops, and writings, he empowers others to explore their inner world, redefine their vision, and create impactful change.

His personal journey is a testament to the power of belief, creativity, and limitless potential. By combining artistic expression, subconscious reprogramming, and business strategy, Chady has developed a unique methodology for unlocking human and entrepreneurial potential.

Now, with *The Next Level*, he shares his most powerful insights; helping you elevate your mindset, embrace transformation, and step into your highest level of success.

Know more about Chady

ABOUT CHADY ELIAS

www.ingramcontent.com/pod-product-compliance
Lightning Source LLC
LaVergne TN
LVHW021510080426
835509LV00018B/2469